Published 1978 by Warwick Press, 730 Fifth Avenue,
New York, New York 10019

First published in Great Britain by Angus and
Robertson, 1977

Copyright © 1977 by Grisewood & Dempsey Ltd

Printed by Mandarin Publishers Ltd, Hong Kong

6 5 4 3 2 1

Library of Congress Catalog No. 77–85260

ISBN 0–531–09087–6
ISBN 0–531–09066–3 library binding

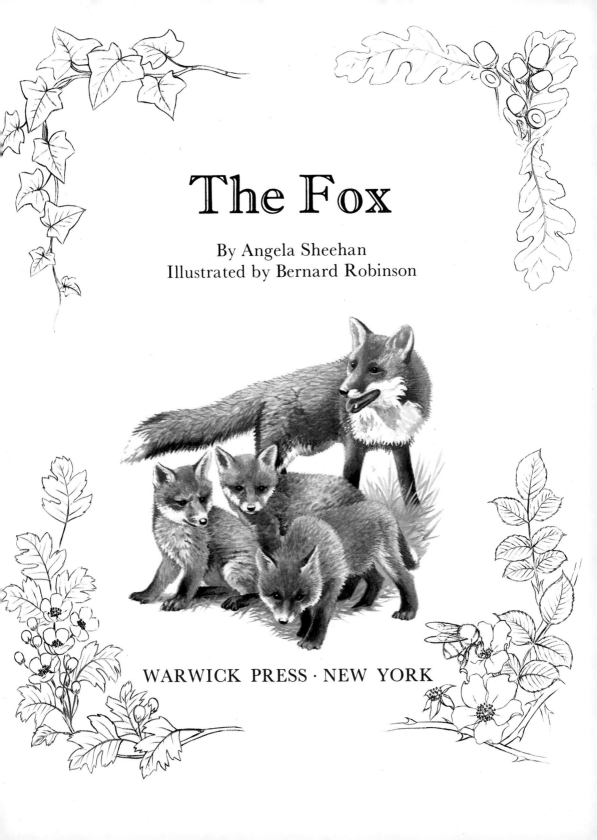

The Fox

By Angela Sheehan
Illustrated by Bernard Robinson

WARWICK PRESS · NEW YORK

The young vixen snuggled deep into a hole.
She wrapped her warm tail around her nose
and floated into a deep sleep. It was her second
day away from home.

During the last two nights she had
traveled a long way. She had crossed fields,
jumped tracks, climbed hills and swum a stream.
Now she was far from the woods where she
was raised.

When she woke it was evening and time to go on. But first she must eat. The night before she had found only some dry bread and bones to eat. Tonight she was near a farm. She could already smell the chickens.

The vixen had seen her mother raid a chicken coop at home, so she knew how. She padded around the wire until she found a small gap. Then she scraped at the ground below and pushed up the wire with her nose. Now there was a big enough space for her to squeeze through.

Once inside, the fox made for the hen house. It was locked. But the fox had no need to open it. For there was a rooster sitting alone and asleep on the roof.

As the fox approached, the chickens inside heard her and started to cluck. The noise woke the rooster and it flapped into the air. The fox leaped at the frightened bird and killed it with one blow of her paw. Then she opened wide her mouth and sank her teeth into its tasty flesh.

After she had eaten the chicken, the fox ran on until she was far beyond the hills. By daybreak she was too tired to go any farther. She had reached a wood just like the one where her mother lived. It would be a good place to make a home.

At the edge of a clearing, the fox found a hole. Inside was a long tunnel. At the end of it was a grass-filled hollow. It made a perfect den, so she moved in. No sooner had she done so, than she heard a noise from another tunnel and smelled an animal coming toward her. She rushed out of the hole. Behind her was an angry badger. He grunted as he chased the stranger from his set. It was not so easy to find a den after all.

Too tired to look any further, the fox
curled up and went to sleep beneath a
hawthorn bush. Grasshoppers jumped high in
the grass. But even their loud chirping could
not keep the sleepy vixen awake.

In the evening the fox explored the woods.
She smelled the flowers, fruits and leaves,
the rabbits and the mice. But the smell she
noticed most was the scent of other foxes.
Each night she followed their tracks by sniffing
places where they left their scent. She could
tell from the scent whether they were vixens or
dog-foxes, and even how old they were.

Though she had no real home of her own,
the fox did not go short of food. She ate
blackberries and the beetles and snails that
crawled in the brambles. She was even quick

enough to catch the insects that hovered among the sweet fruit.

Each day she became a more skillful hunter. She tracked her prey slowly and silently. She never allowed the wind to carry her scent toward the victim. When she was near enough, she pounced and killed swiftly. One of her favorite treats was to eat frogs by the stream at night.

One night she tried to catch a hedgehog. But she did not know how to unroll the prickly creature. She tried hard but her only reward was a sore paw.

After a while the weather became too cold for the fox to sleep just anywhere. She needed a home. So she found an old fox hole, near a rabbit warren.

First she had to clear the garbage left by the last fox. There were old bones and scraps and feathers everywhere.

Once she had moved into the hole, she explored the area around her home. She wanted to know every part of it. And she wanted the other foxes to know that she lived there, too. She took the same route night after night. As she went she marked certain tree stumps and clumps of grass with her scent. The other foxes would know from the smell, when she had passed by.

Now that she had a home of her own, the vixen could have some cubs. First she needed a mate. She knew where all the other foxes lived. At night she heard them barking and often barked in reply. But she never really came close to any of them. So now she began to howl even louder to let them know she wanted a mate.

At first only a few farm dogs came. But then a dog-fox heard her wails. Even though his den was far away, he hurried to answer her call.

Every night he came to her. The two foxes played together until they trusted each other enough to mate.

After they had mated, the two foxes
stayed in their separate homes. But they still
saw each other in the woods.

Food was hard to find now. In spring and
summer there were insects and birds' eggs
to eat. There were also young animals, too
weak to escape from the foxes. But by winter
the animals were fully grown; most of the
insects were dead; the frogs were asleep
underground; and the mice were hidden in
their burrows.

The fox had to be brave as well as cunning to catch her food. She caught rabbits by pretending to play harmlessly near them and then pouncing on them. She attacked deer twice her size; and stole ducks and geese from the farm.

Then spring came. The vixen's cubs were born just seven weeks after she had mated. The first flowers were blooming in the woods. But the young cubs could not see them. Their eyes were still shut. Their mother gave them milk, washed them, and kept them warm.

The vixen did not leave her cubs when they were first born. But she did not go hungry. Her mate brought her food. He also brought some for the cubs as they grew bigger.

Before they were a month old, the four cubs went outside for the first time. Their mother guarded them closely. She kept her ears and nose alert for any danger. The cubs loved to run about and play together. They loved to see all the new sights, smell all the new smells and hear all the new sounds.

Every evening they went out to play.
They chased flies, attacked feathers in the
wind, pounced on each other and fought for
bones. One of their favorite games was trying
to catch their mother's tail as she whipped
it from side to side.

As they grew older, they learned more games. Instead of giving their food to them, their mother hid it. The cubs had to sniff it out for themselves. The smallest cub never found the food first. And so he became hungry. The others became more and more clever.

But they were still too young to go far into the woods. Their mother watched them all the time. One bark from her would bring them all running back to the safety of the hole. The mother fox only went out to hunt herself when the cubs were asleep. And she made sure that no enemies followed her home.

But the fox's home was too near the rabbit warren to be safe. Often men came from the farm to shoot the rabbits. The sound of the guns frightened the cubs. It frightened their mother too. So she left the hole and took the family deeper into the wood.

She found a hole on the edge of the badgers' set. The badgers no longer used the hole so they did not mind the fox family moving in. Within days the badgers' set began to look a mess. The tidy badgers always cleared their garbage. But the foxes left theirs scattered everywhere.

When they were two months old, the
cubs went hunting with their mother. They had
a lot to learn. There were many different
animals to catch, and different ways to catch
them. They soon learned where to find birds'
nests and how to steal the eggs. Only the
small cub made mistakes. He always chased
the mother bird as it flew away, instead of
eating the eggs like the others. He would
never be a good hunter.

The others could soon catch rabbits and
voles, and even fast-moving mice. They had
learned to pounce with their paws, not with
their jaws.

One evening the small cub went out all alone to find food. He heard buzzing coming from some foxgloves and went to look. The flowers were covered in bumblebees. They smelled so good that the hungry cub tried to eat them. But they turned out not to be so tasty. One by one they stung the cub on the nose. He squealed and ran home to his mother as fast as he could. He would never be big and brave like the others.

But the cub could not live with his mother forever. Soon the other three cubs left home. They were ready to start a new life as their mother had done one year before. It was time, too, for the smallest fox to go. He must take his chance and learn to watch out for himself.

So the young cub left last of all. His mother was tired after bringing up her family. She needed a rest before she had her next family.

More About Foxes

The fox in the story is the red fox. It lives in North America, Europe and parts of Asia. Other foxes live in other parts of the world. The arctic fox has a white coat to match the snowy land in which it lives. The small sandy colored fennec fox lives in the desert.

Where Foxes Live

Foxes do not have a particular home except when they are breeding. During the summer they sleep anywhere. In winter they find (never dig) an underground home. The fox lays claim to the surrounding area by marking "posts" with a strong odor mixed in with its urine. They communicate with each other by exchanging barks and leaving scent messages.

Cunning as a Fox

The fox is famous for its cunning, especially for the way it "charms" rabbits. It leaps about playfully near them and shows no sign of having seen them. The watching rabbits cannot take their eyes off the dancing fox. Then suddenly the fox pounces.

Unlike rabbits, farmers know all about the fox's cunning. They know that it will attack newborn lambs and kill every hen in a coop if it can

Ears The fox can hear better than a dog. An alert fox has its ears pricked.

Nose The fox's sense of smell is very keen.Its wet nose enables it to tell which way the wind is blowing, so it knows where a smell is coming from.

Teeth Long ones at the front for tearing meat and sharp side ones for slicing it.

Eyes Not as important as nose and ears, but fox can see movement well at night. Look at the photograph on the opposite page.

Tail The fox's tail is called a brush. It helps the fox balance. The fox also uses it to signal to other foxes. At night, it uses it like a scarf to keep warm.

Legs Strong legs and feet for running. The fox can run far at a steady speed.

The body of a red fox

A family of fox cubs, their eyes lit up by the flash of a camera.

Keeping Watch

It is easy to find where foxes live because they leave so many clues. Outside any fox hole you will find the remains of their food. The tracks they make and the "posts" they mark are easy to find and follow. You can track them from their dung too. But remember that the fox can hear and smell you coming long before you can see it. So, if you want to see a fox you must be patient.

get in. That is why farmers shoot foxes.

But foxes do not always kill for food. More and more foxes now come into towns to scavenge garbage. When foxes find more food than they can eat, they sometimes bury some.

Tally Ho

This is the cry of the huntsman as he sets off with horses and hounds to chase and kill a single fox. People have hunted in this way, wearing special pink (red) coats, for centuries. Today most people would like fox hunting to be banned.

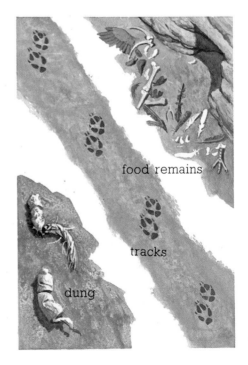

food remains

tracks

dung

Some things to look for when tracking a fox.